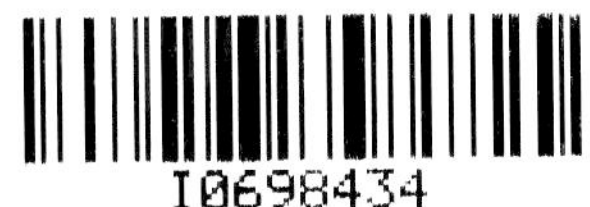

This Book Belongs To

____

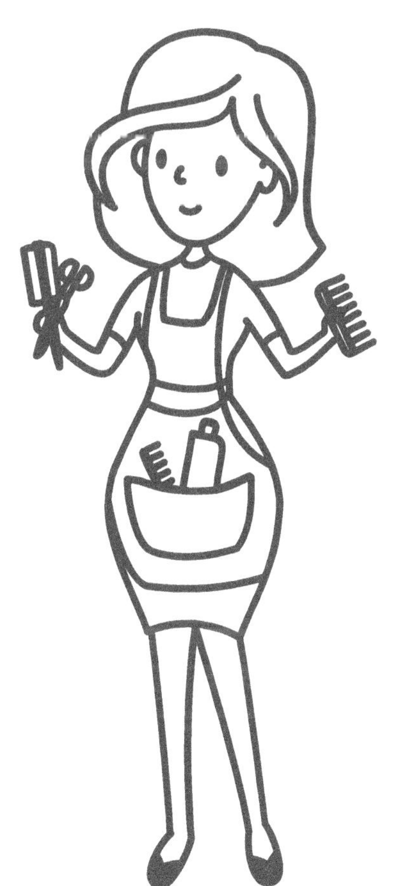

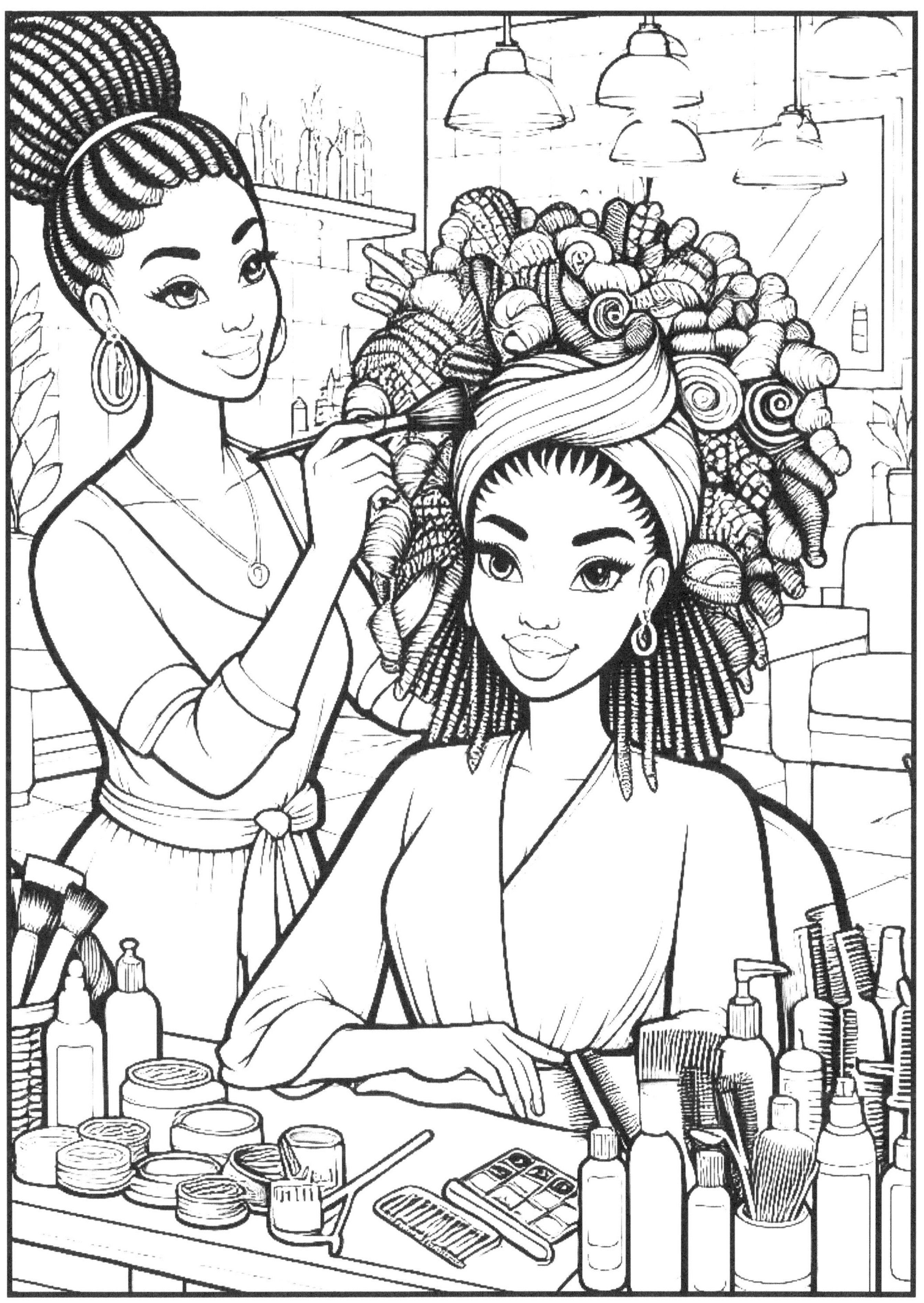

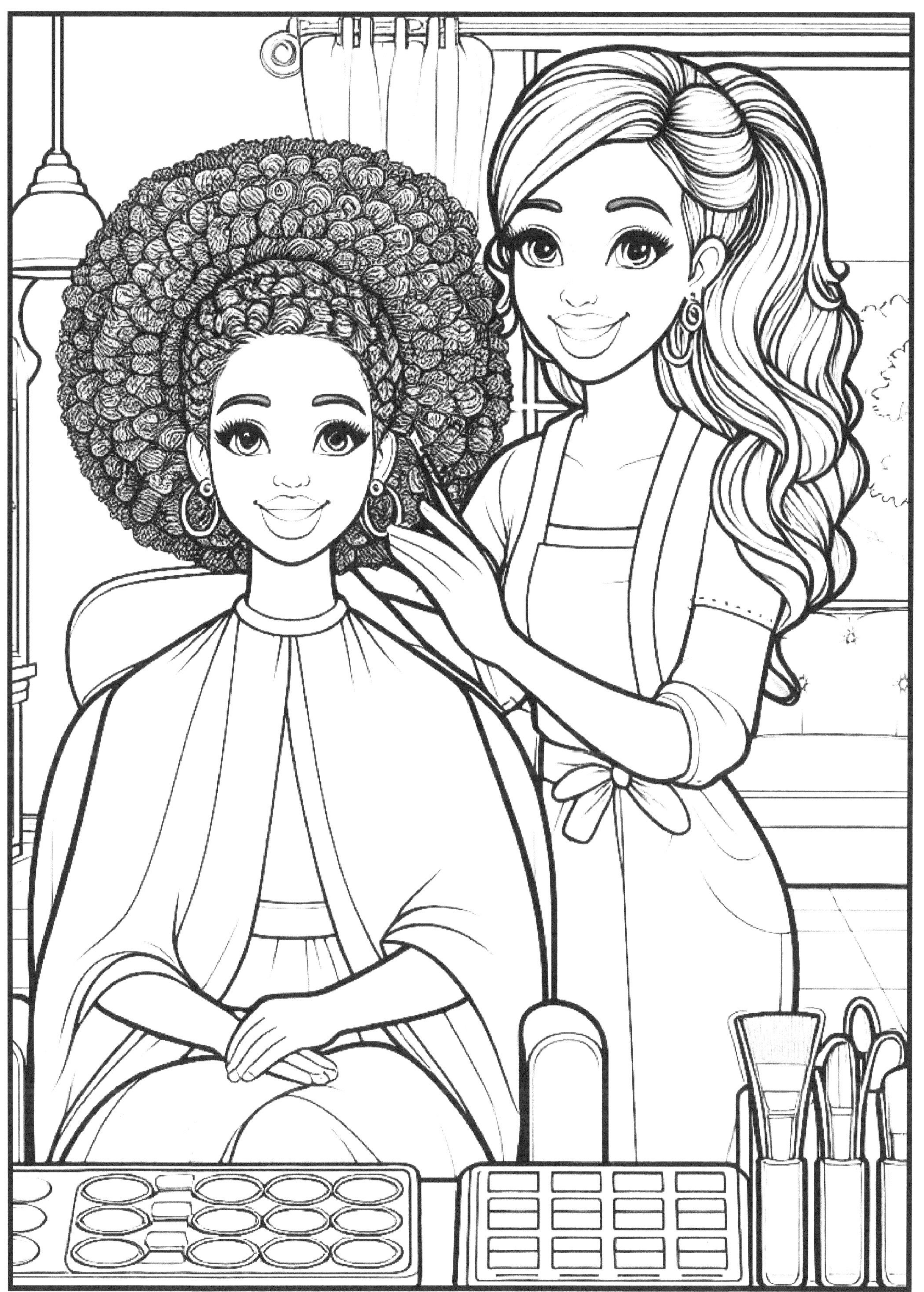

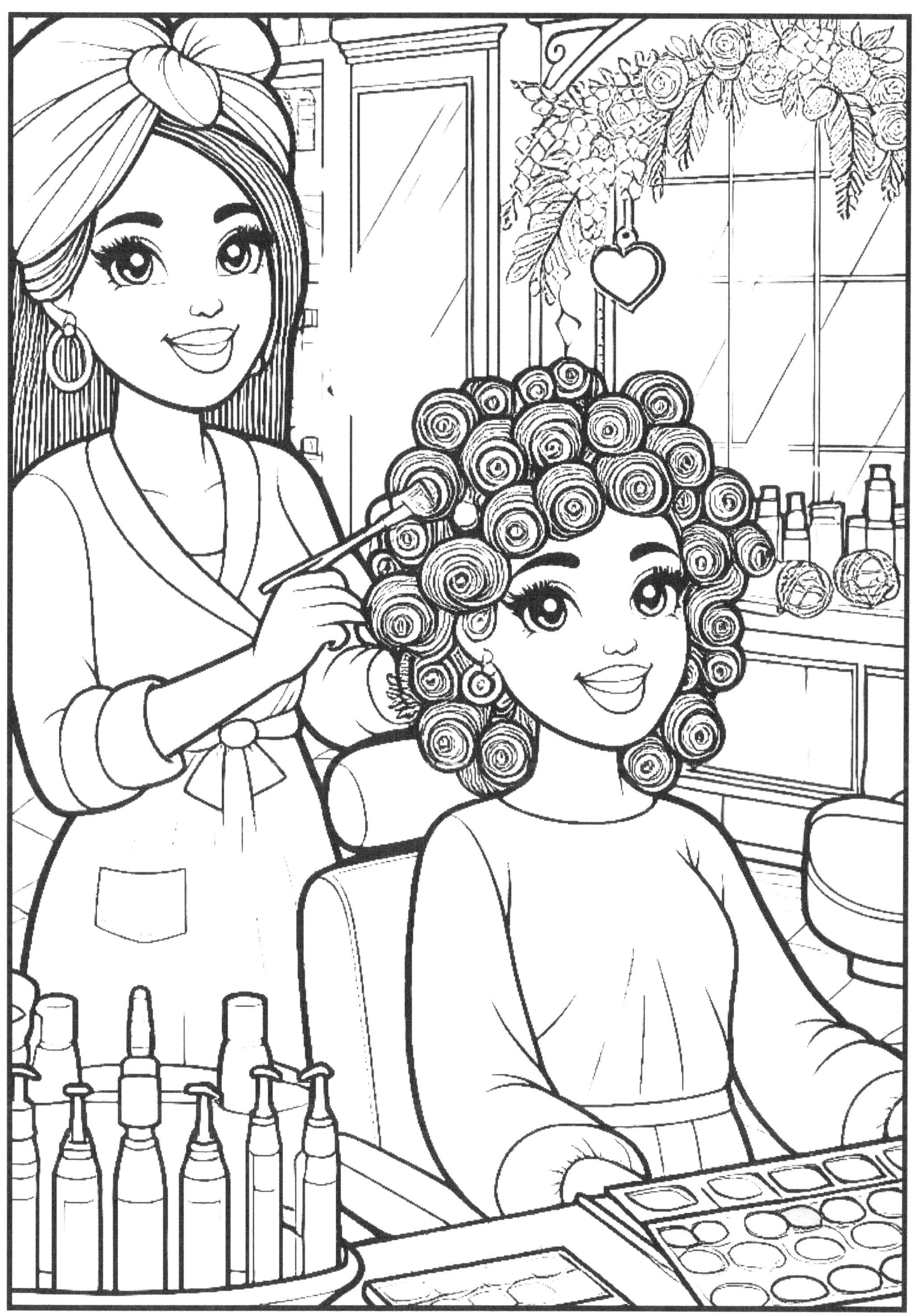

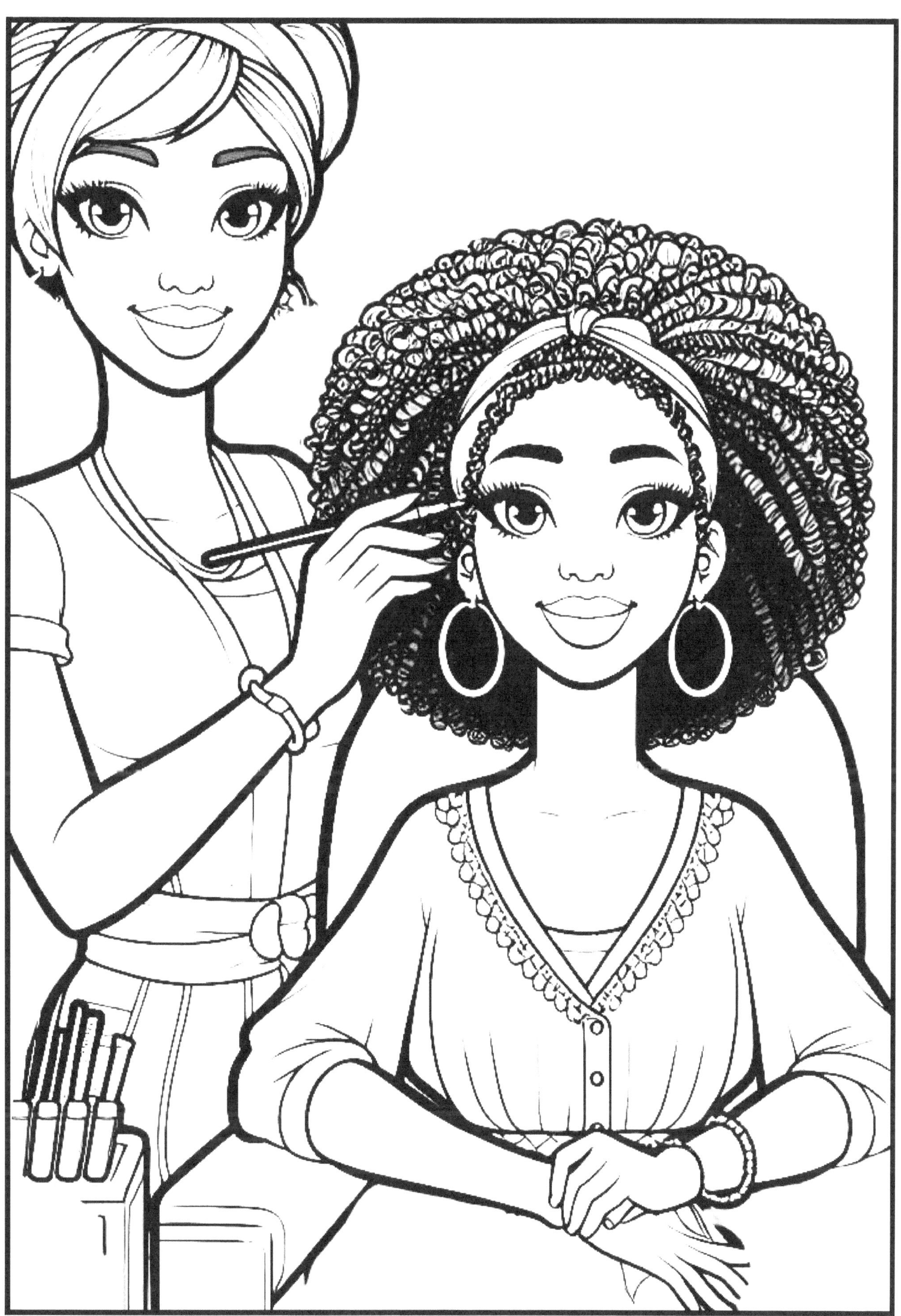

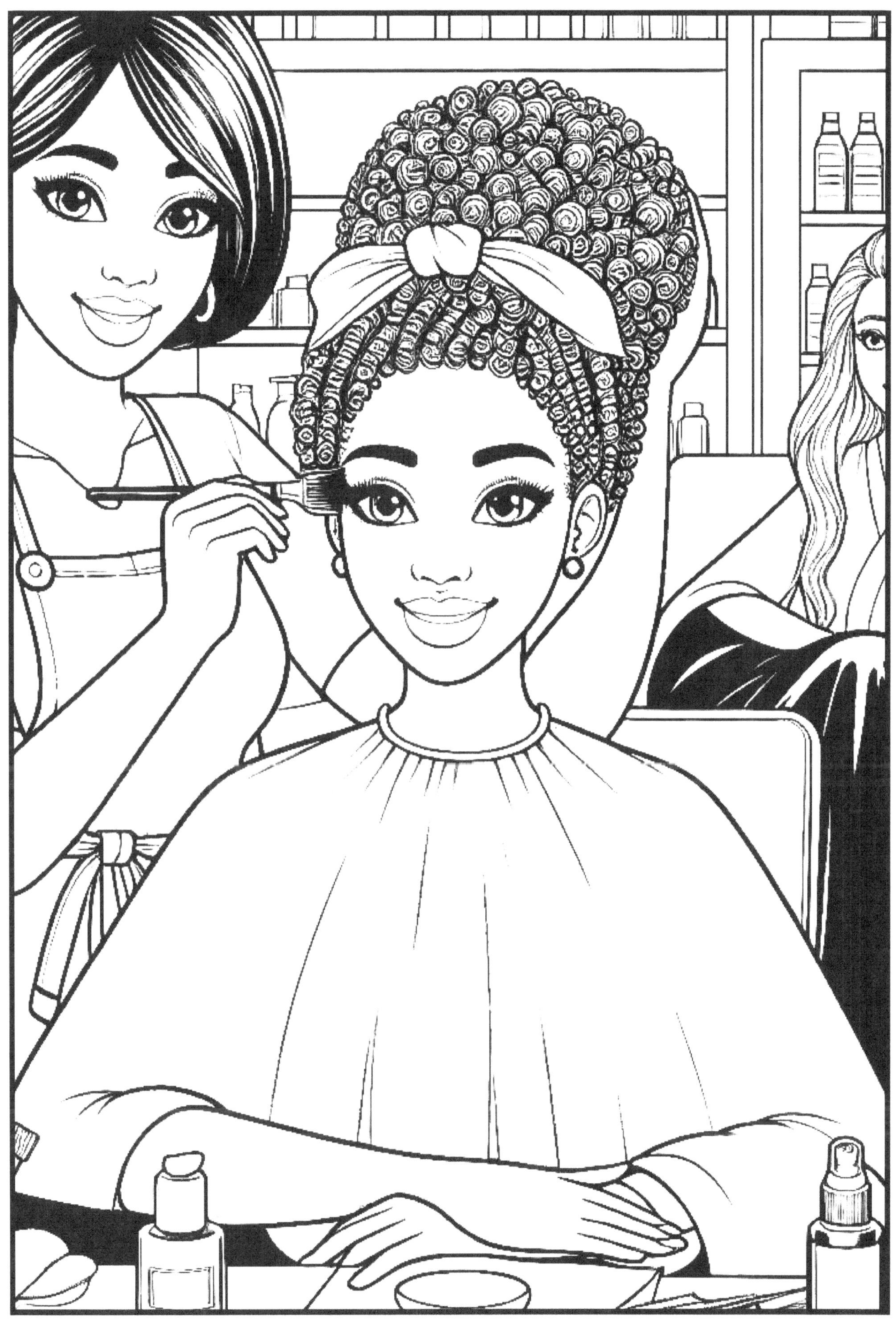

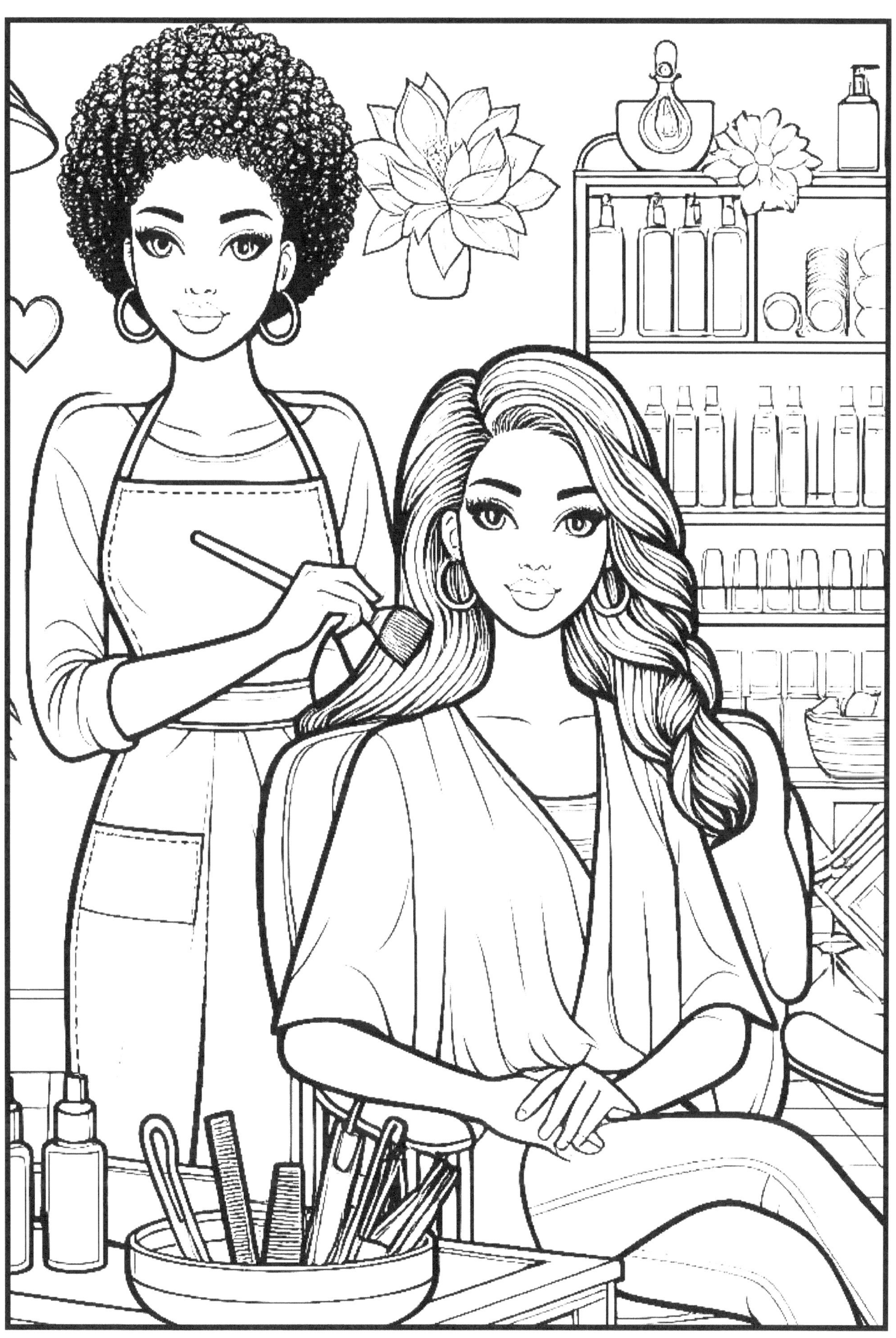

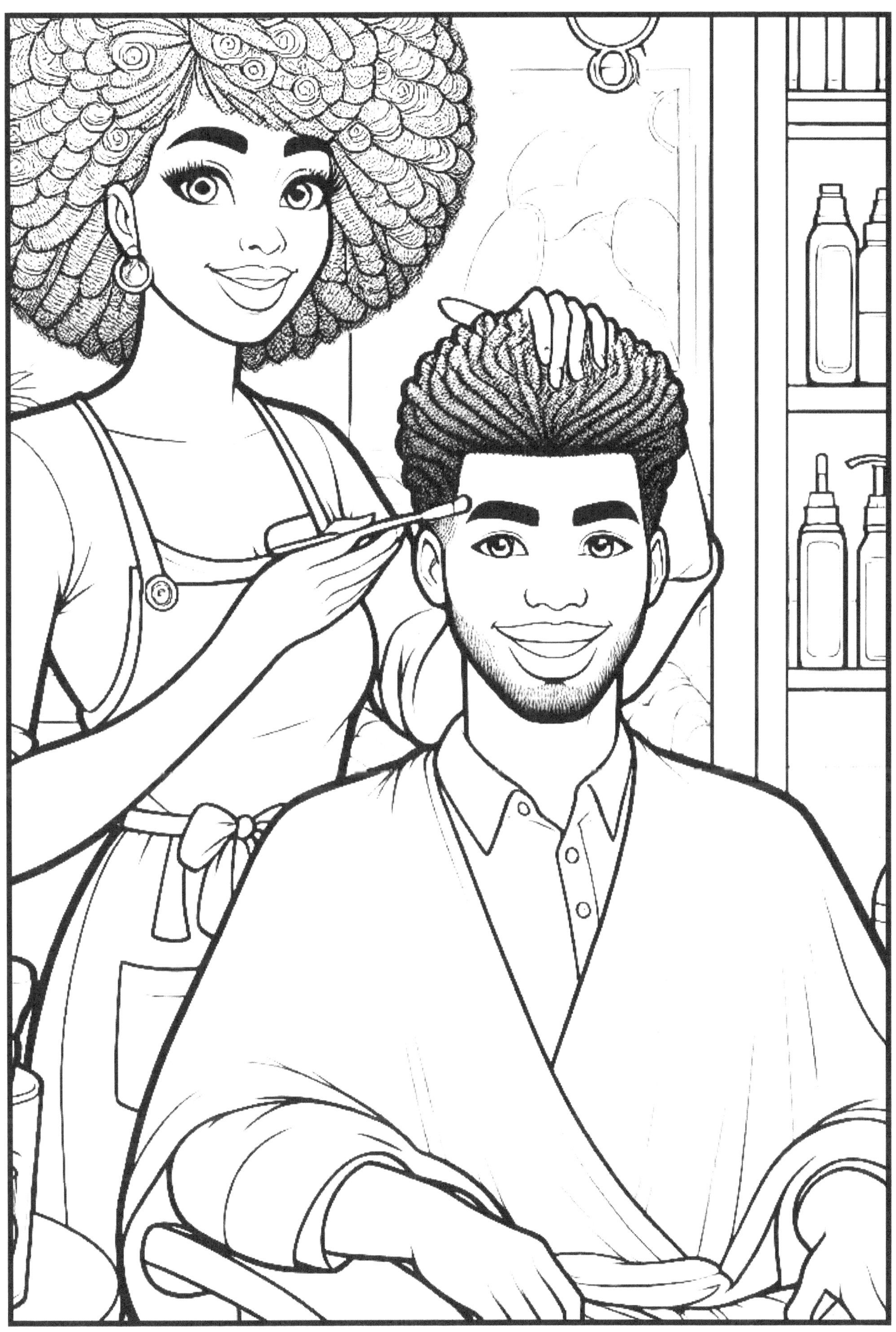

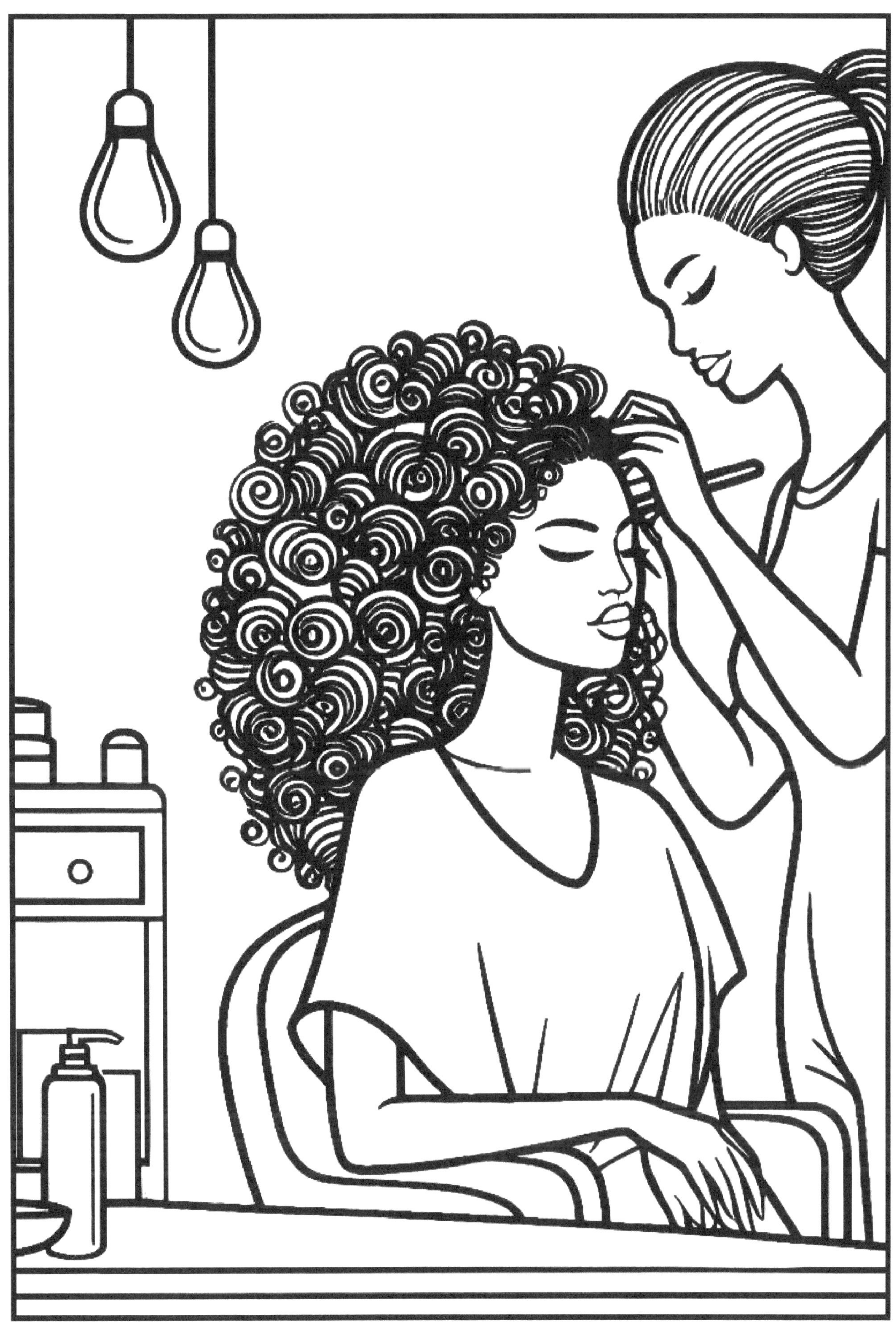

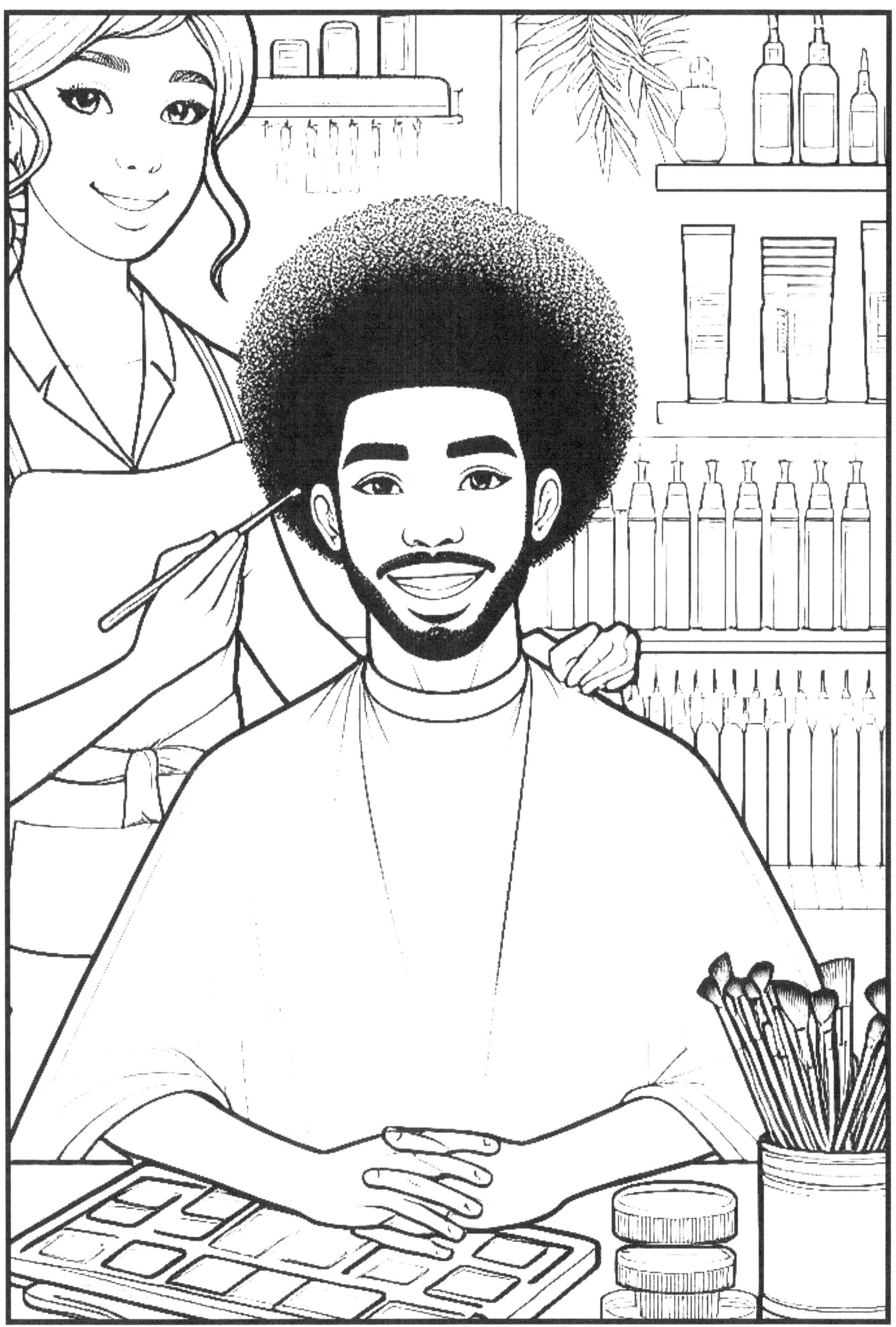

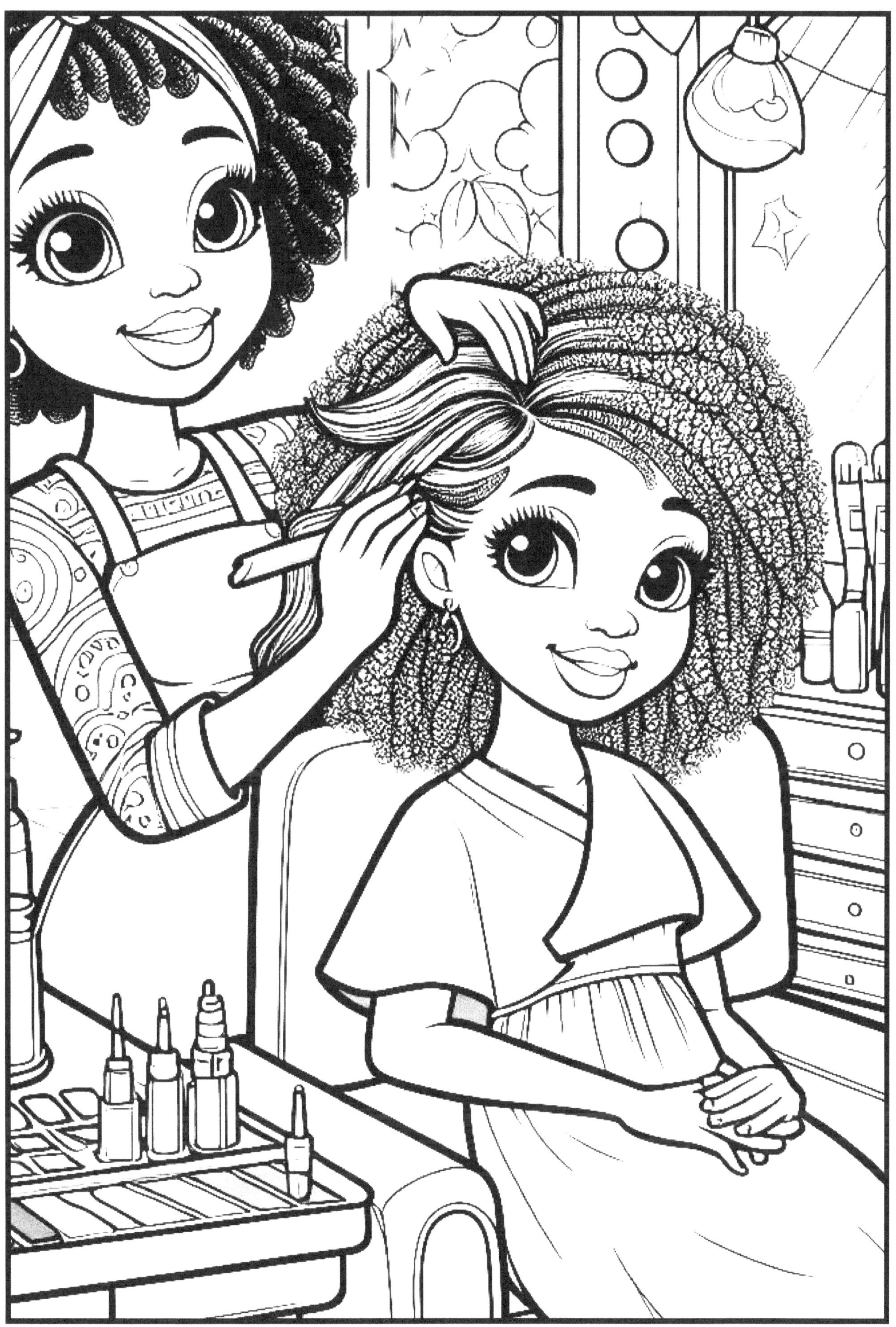

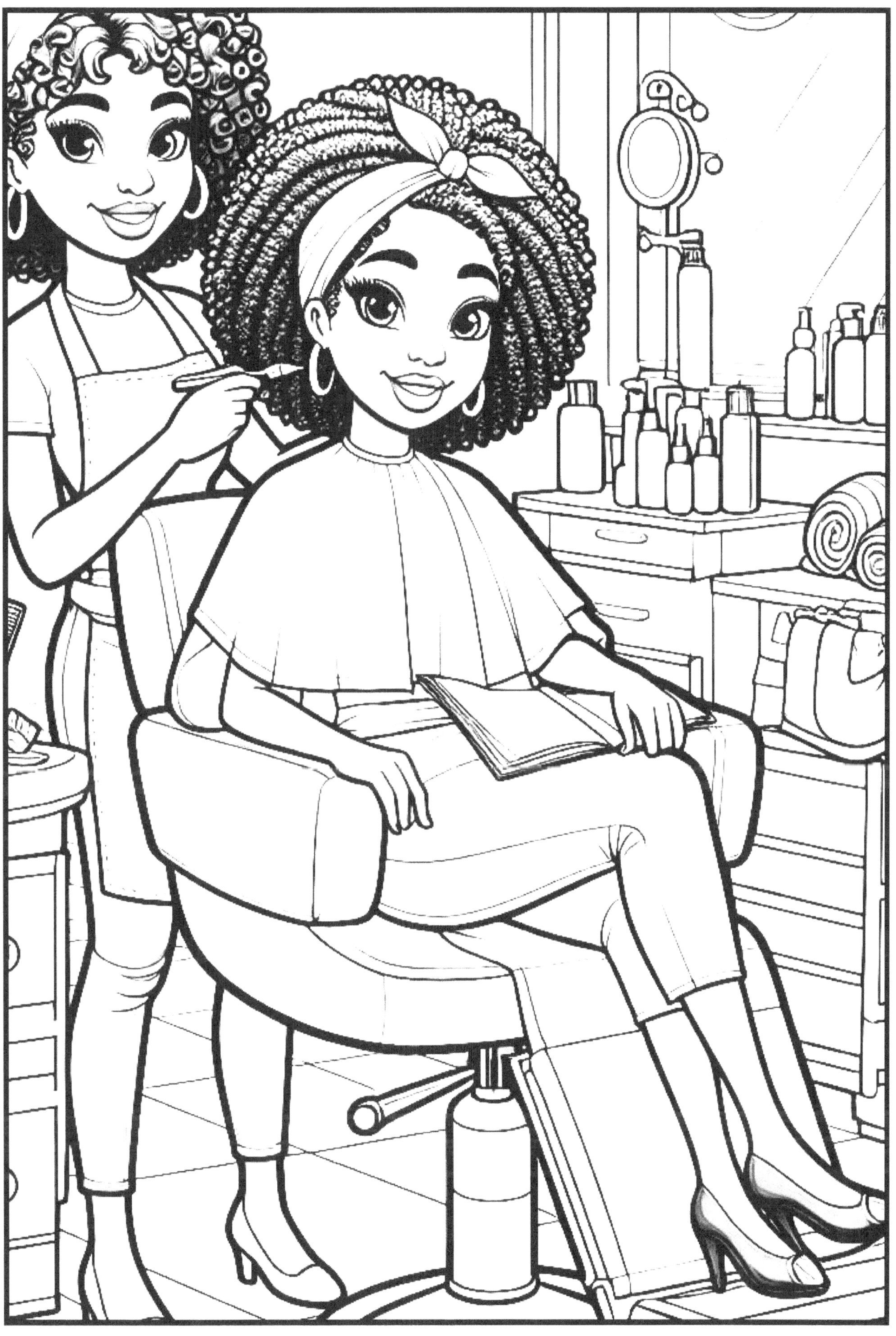

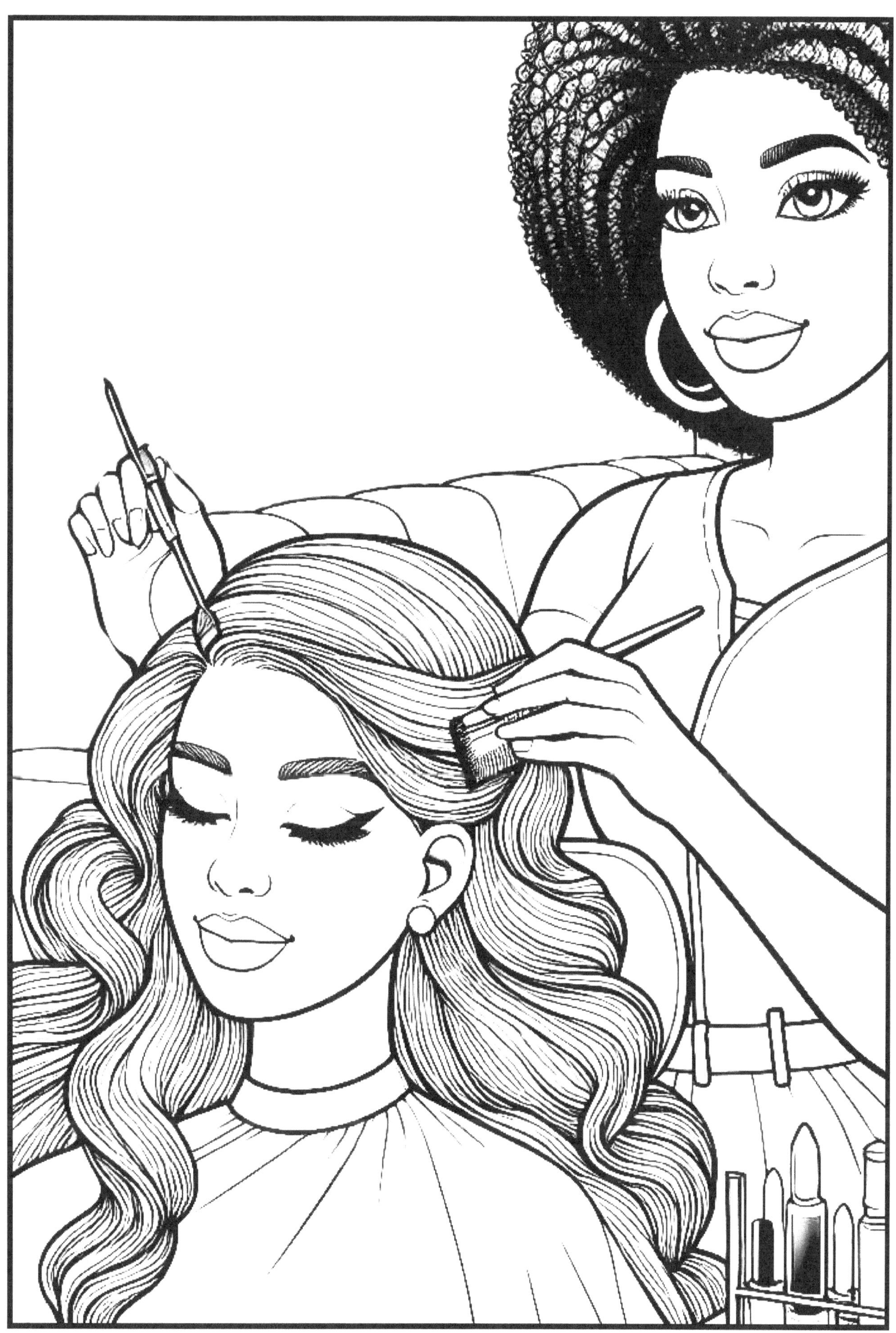

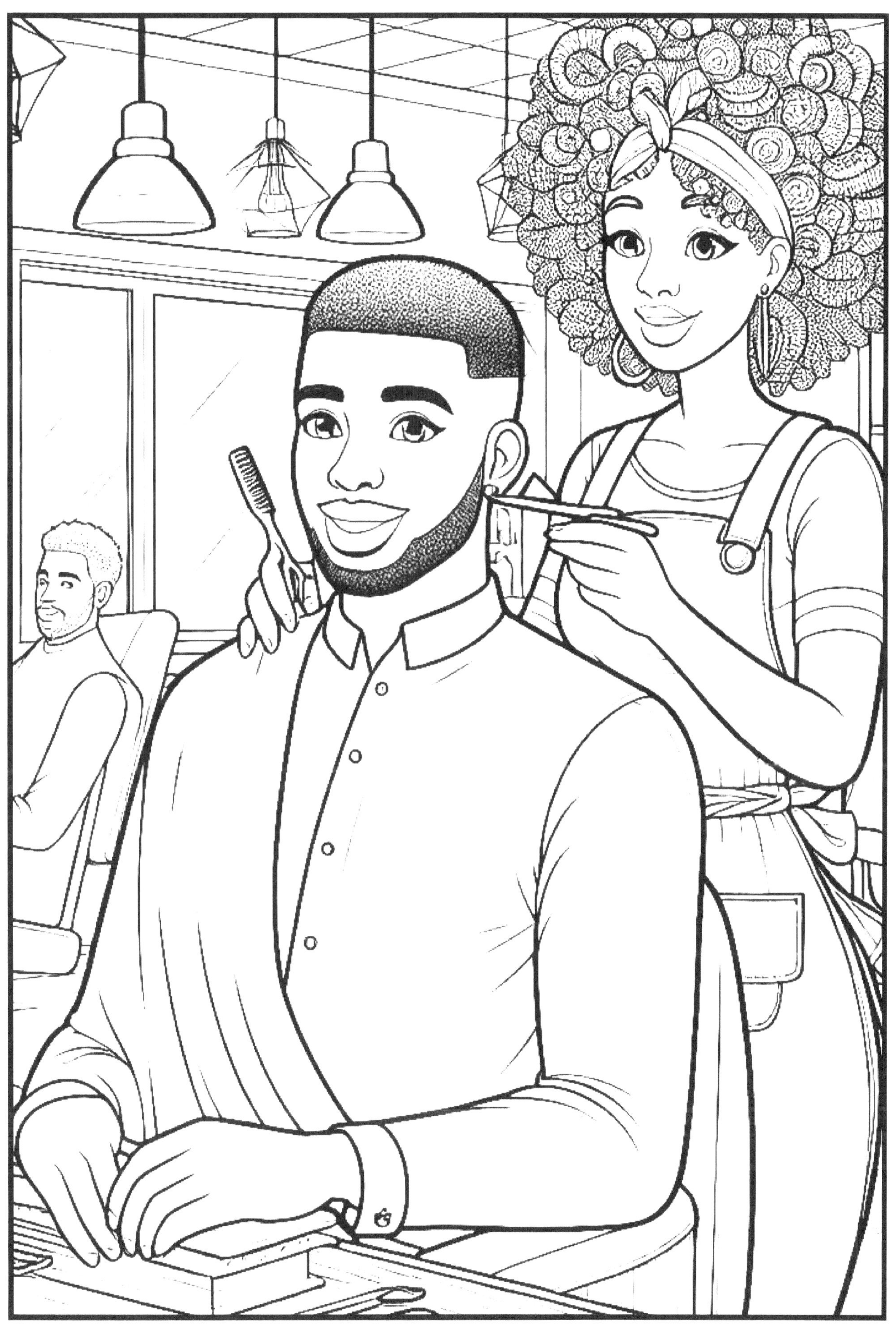

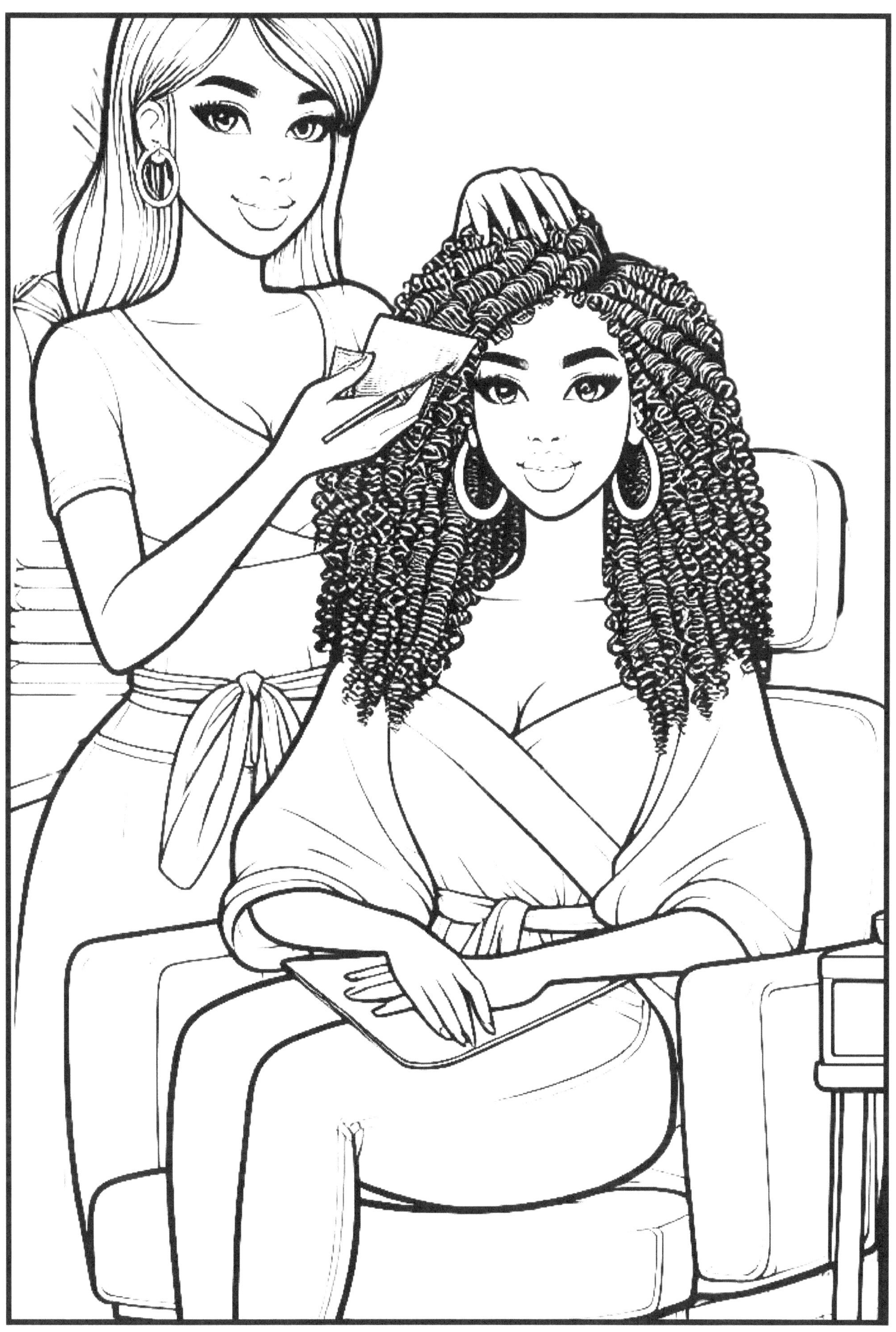

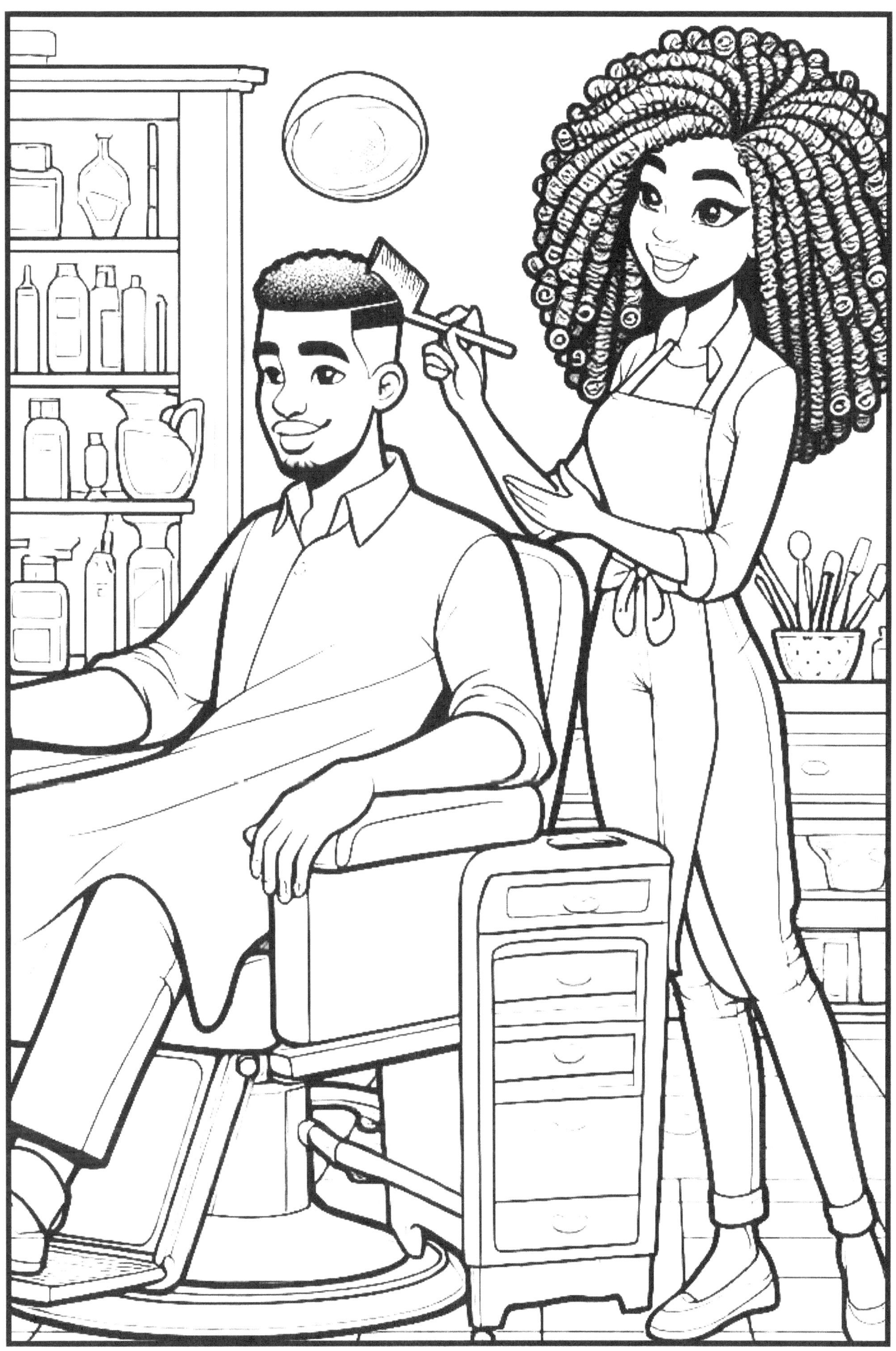

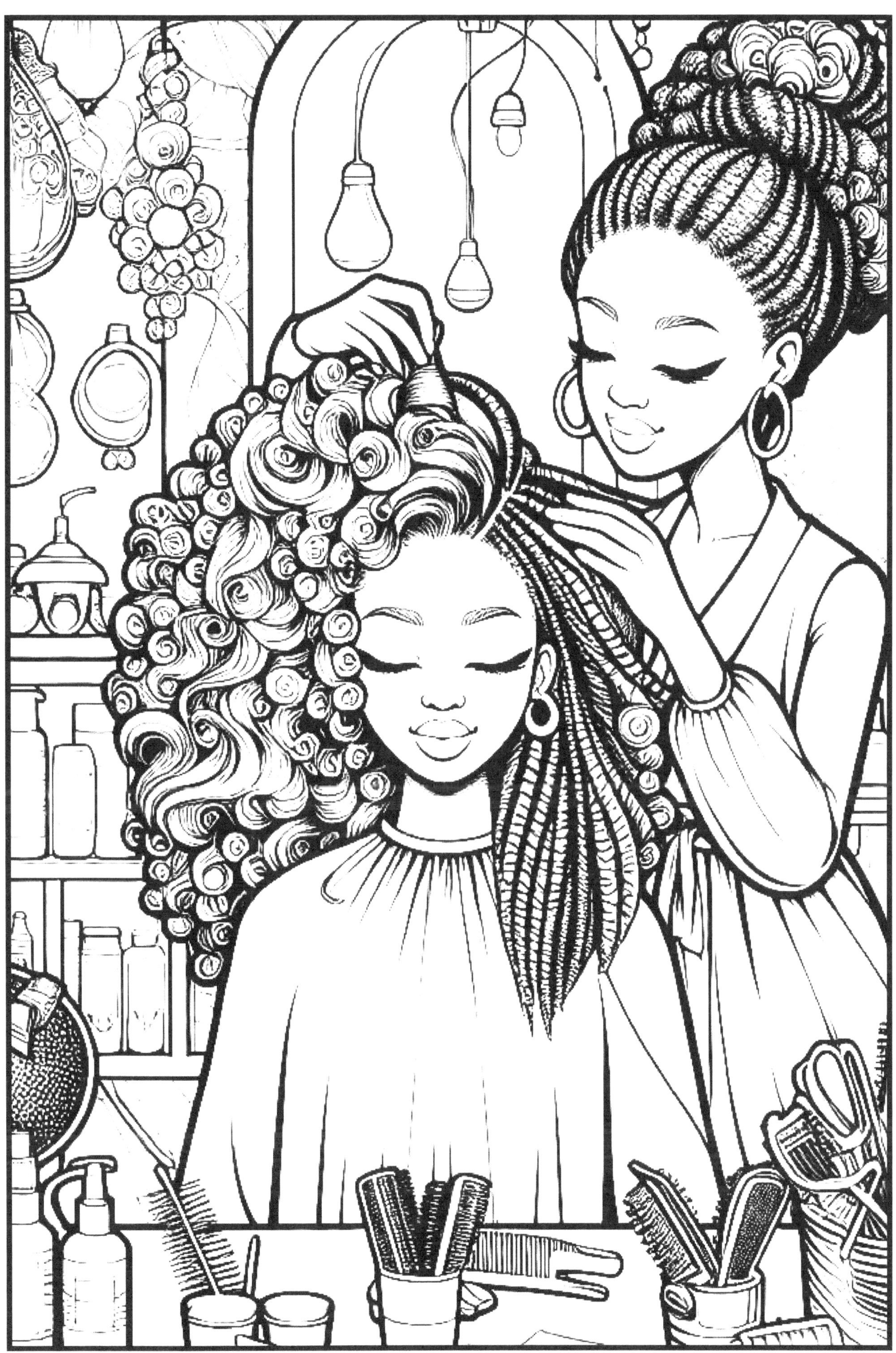

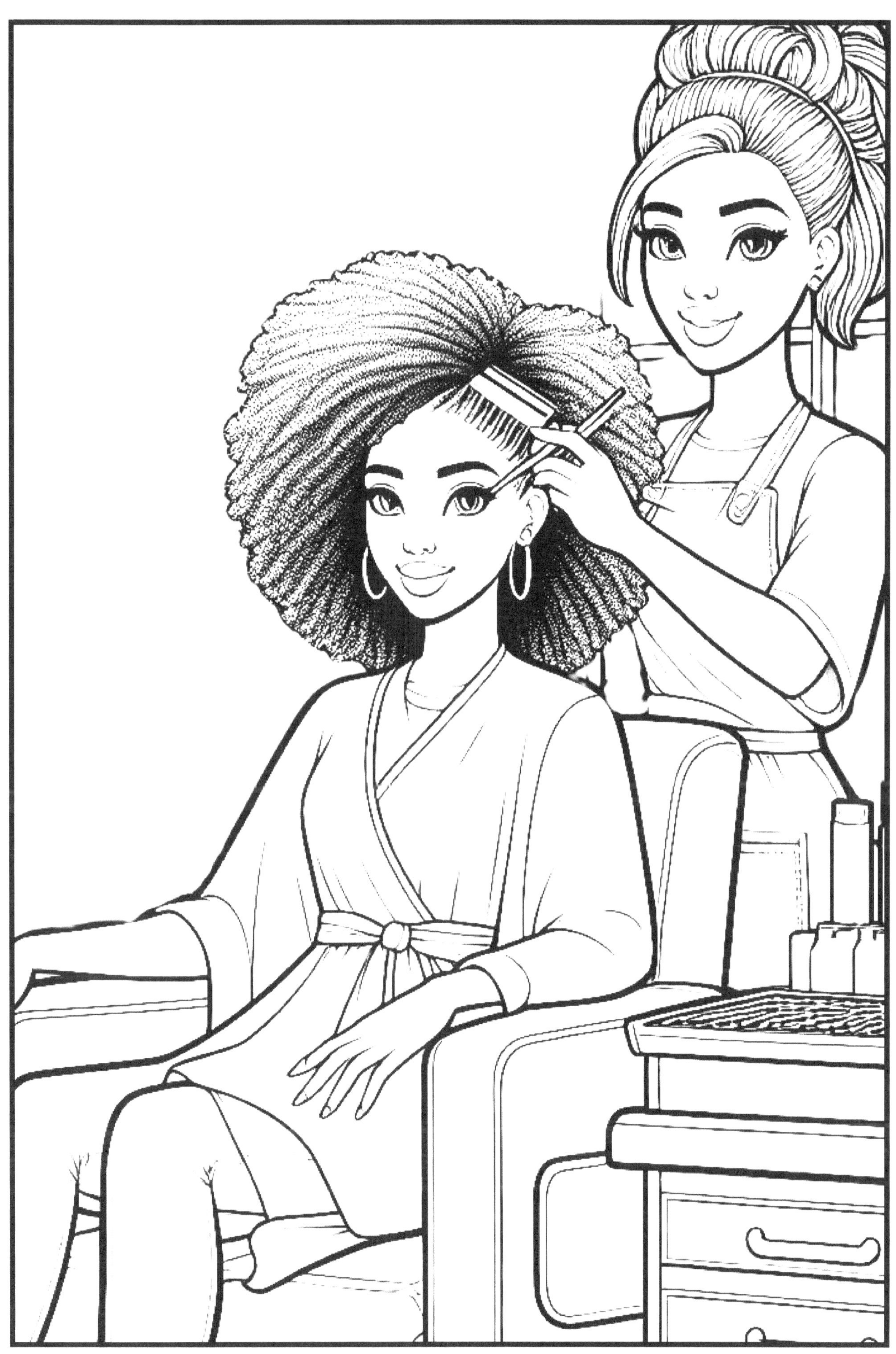

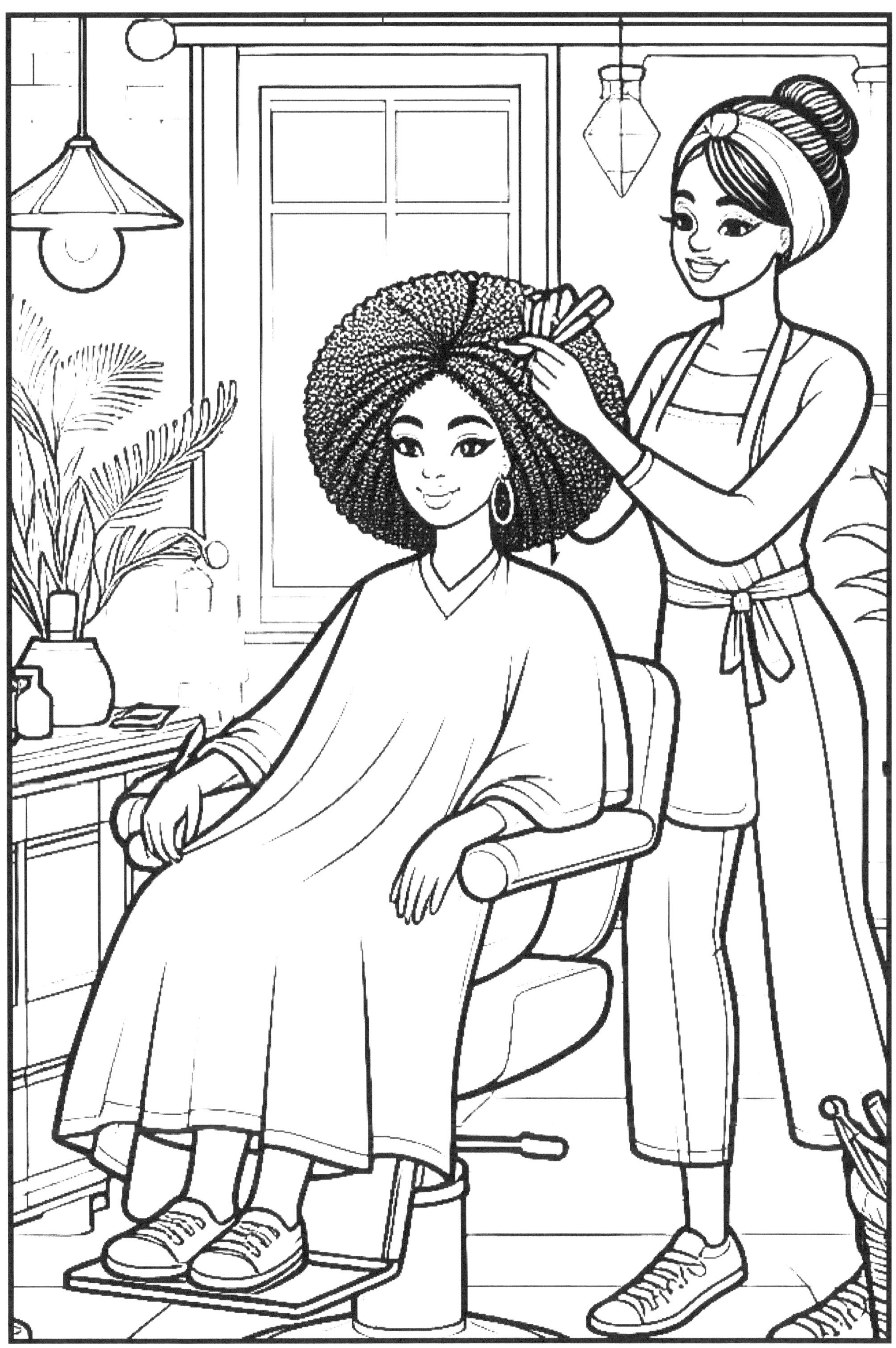

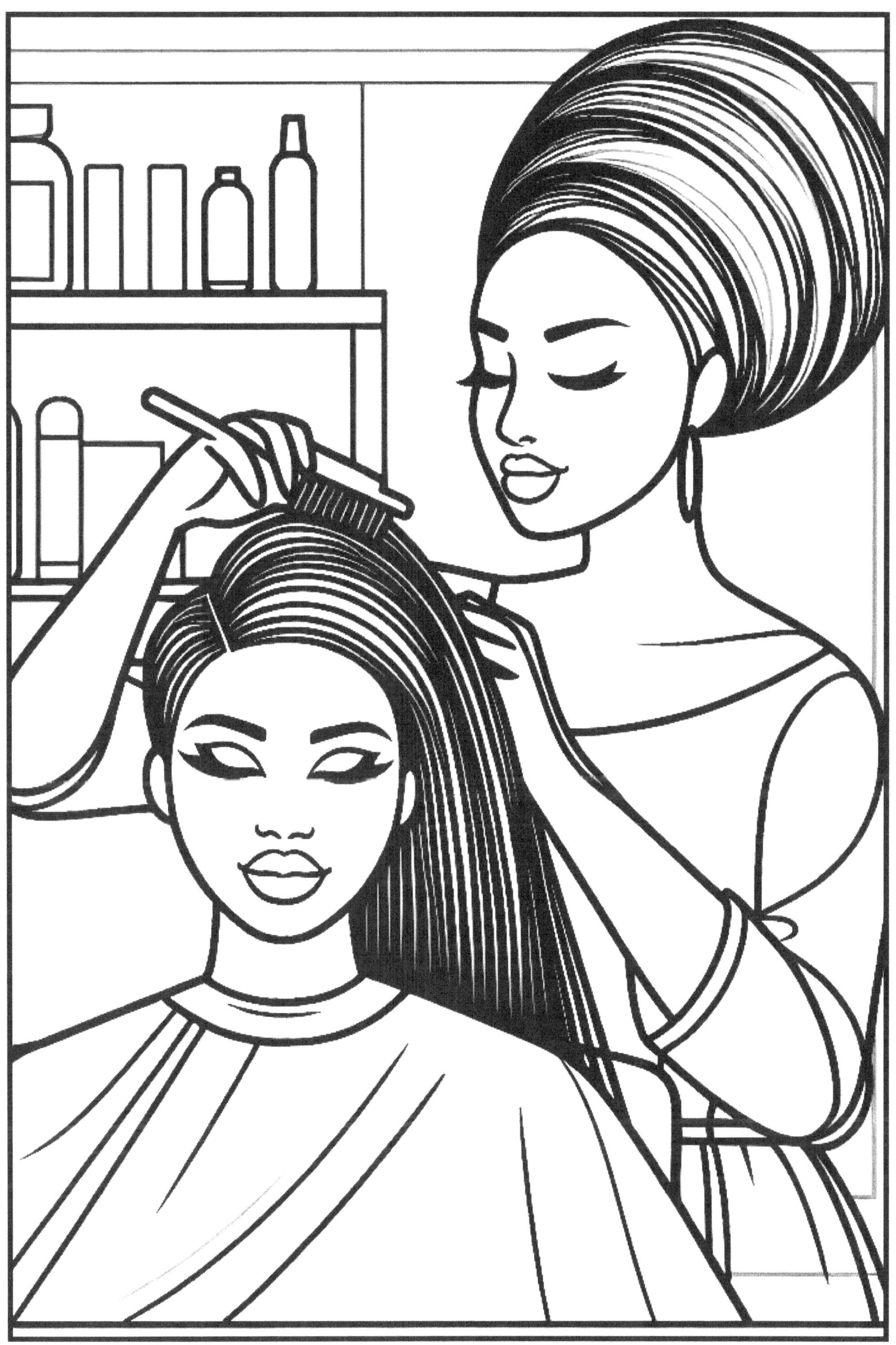

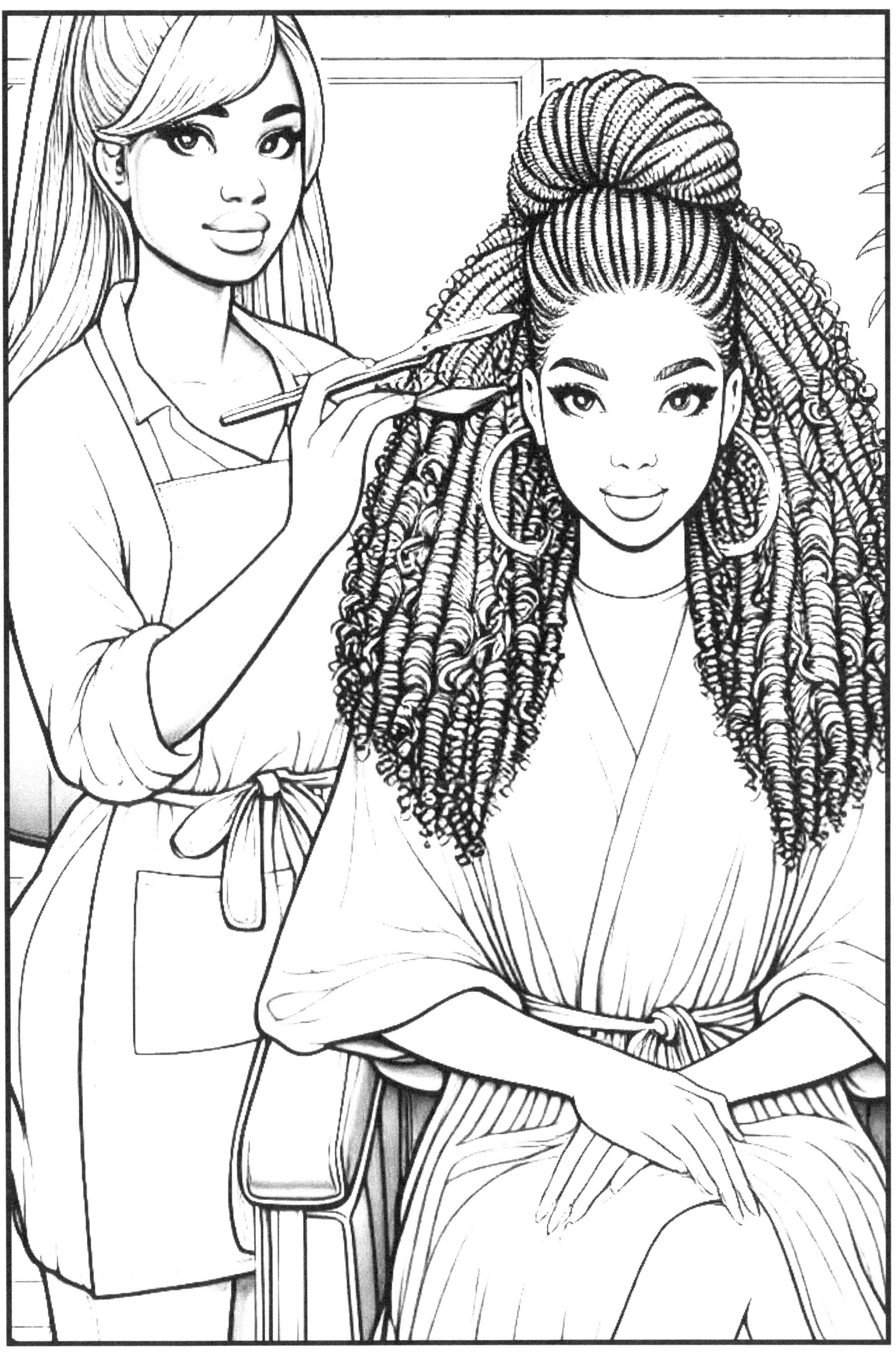

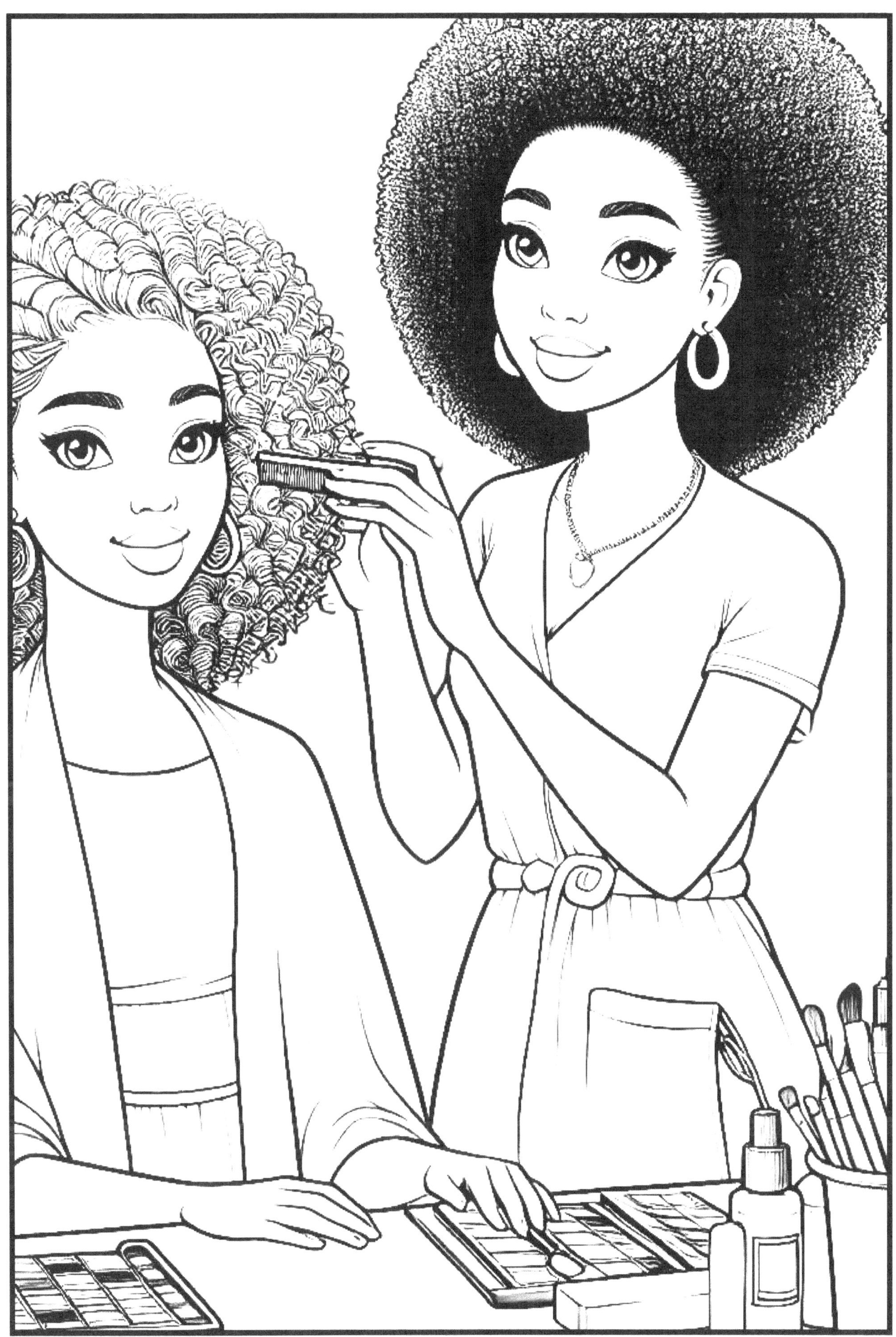

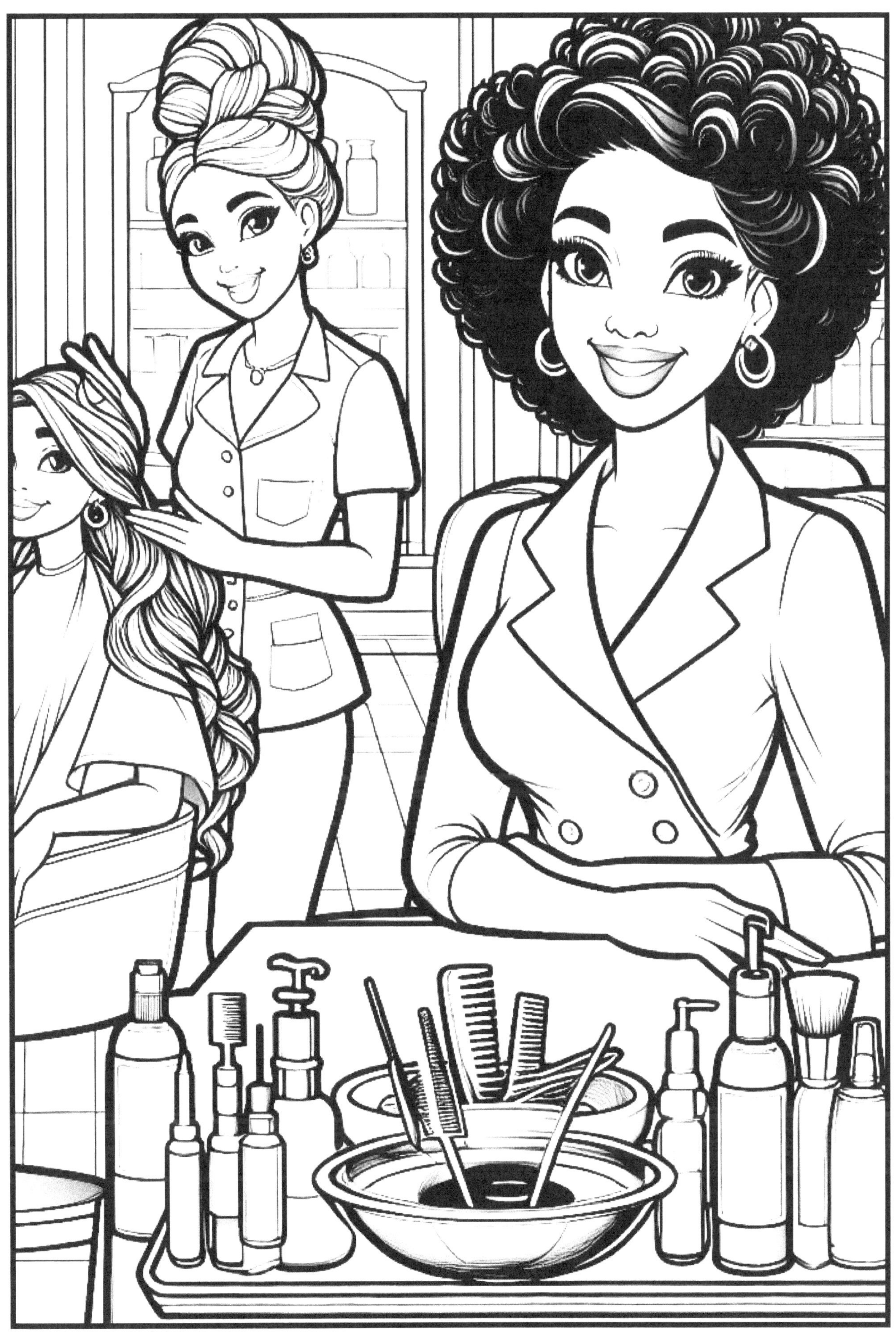

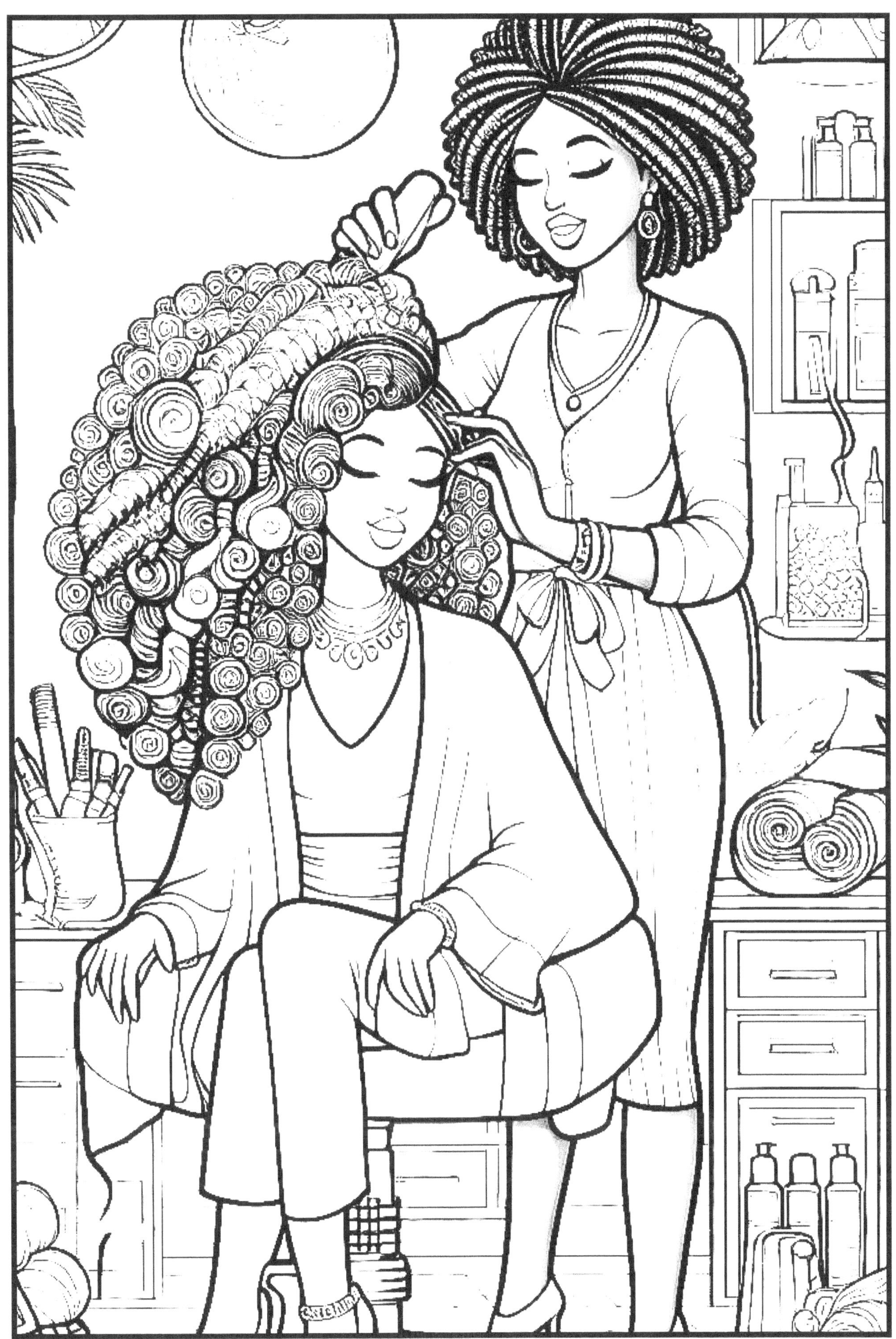

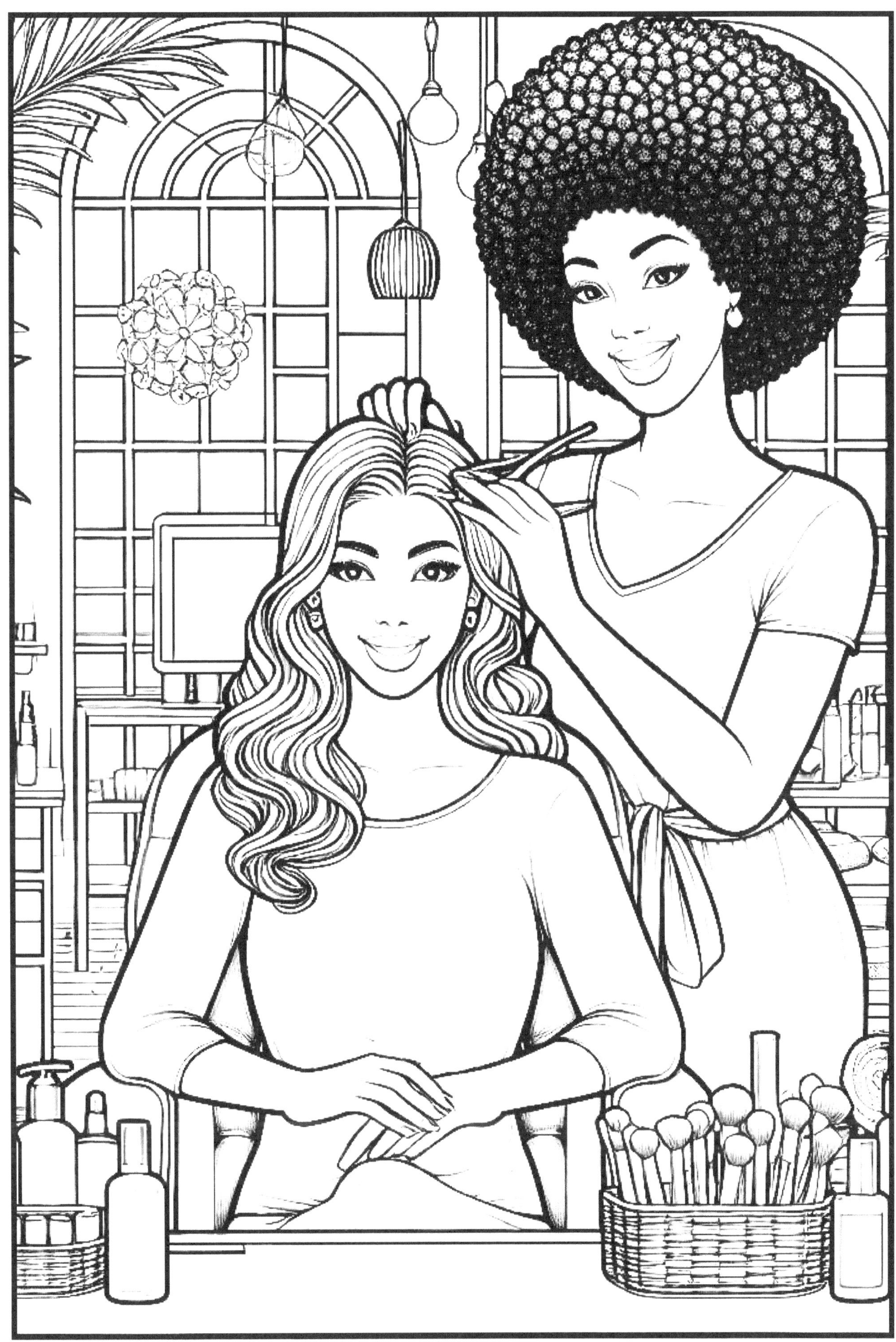